Networking for Success

The Art of Establishing Personal Contacts

Nancy Flynn

A Fifty-Minute™ Series Book

Networking for Success

The Art of Establishing Personal Contacts

Nancy Flynn

CREDITS:
Senior Editor: **Debbie Woodbury**
Editor: **Ann Gosch**
Assistant Editor: **Genevieve Del Rosario**
Production Manager: **Judy Petry**
Design: **Nicole Phillips**
Production Artist: **Rich Lehl**
Cartoonist: **Ralph Mapson**

© 2003 by Nancy Flynn
Printed in the United States of America by Von Hoffmann Graphics, Inc.

www.crisplearning.com

03 04 05 06   10 9 8 7 6 5 4 3 2 1

Library of Congress Catalog Card Number 2002116813
Flynn, Nancy
Networking for Success
ISBN 1-56052-682-3

Learning Objectives For:

NETWORKING FOR SUCCESS

The objectives for *Networking for Success* are listed below. They have been developed to guide you, the reader, to the core issues covered in this book.

THE OBJECTIVES OF THIS BOOK ARE:

❑ 1) To provide a comprehensive understanding of networking—what it is, what it is not, and why it is so important to career and personal growth.

❑ 2) To highlight the role of focus in defining networking goals and creating a strategic action plan for success.

❑ 3) To present the fundamentals of successful networking: building and growing a network, nurturing relationships with key influencers, and refining your professional presence.

❑ 4) To explore traditional networking tools and techniques, as well as the additional networking opportunities of e-mail and the Internet.

❑ 5) To explain strategies for overcoming networking challenges and roadblocks that can derail career success.

ASSESSING YOUR PROGRESS

In addition to the learning objectives, Crisp Learning has developed an **assessment** that covers the fundamental information presented in this book. A 25-item, multiple-choice and true-false questionnaire allows the reader to evaluate his or her comprehension of the subject matter. To buy the assessment and answer key, go to www.crisplearning.com and search on the book title, or call 1-800-442-7477.

Assessments should not be used in any employee selection process.

About the Author

Author, speaker, and consultant Nancy Flynn is an internationally recognized expert in electronic and traditional business communications. The author of several books including *Writing Effective E-Mail* (Crisp Publications), *The ePolicy Handbook, E-Mail Rules* and *The $100,000 Writer,* Ms. Flynn is a popular keynote speaker and seminar leader for corporations, associations, and government entities. Recognized for her expertise, Ms. Flynn has been featured by *The Wall Street Journal, US News & World Report,* USAtoday.com, National Public Radio, *Woman's Day,* and other national and international media outlets. For more information, visit her Web site at www.WriteToBusiness.com.

Ms. Flynn is founder and executive director of The ePolicy Institute, www.ePolicyInstitute.com, an organization devoted to helping employers reduce electronic liabilities, while helping employees enhance their e-mail writing and management skills. Through the ePolicy Institute Speakers' Bureau, Ms. Flynn conducts e-mail writing, e-mail management, and e-policy seminars worldwide. *Networking for Success* workshops and keynote speeches based on the material presented in this book are available. Please contact Ms. Flynn for information:

Nancy Flynn
Author, Speaker, and Consultant
Executive Director, The ePolicy Institute
2300 Walhaven Court, Suite 200A
Columbus, OH 43220
Toll Free: 800-292-7332
Phone: 614-451-3200
Fax: 614-451-8726
E-mail: Nancy@WriteToBusiness.com
www.WriteToBusiness.com
E-mail: Nancy@ePolicyInstitute.com
www.ePolicyInstitute.com

How to Use This Book

A Crisp Learning *Fifty-Minute™ Book* can be used in a variety of ways. Individual self-study is one of the most common. However, many organizations use *Fifty-Minute* books for pre-study before a classroom training session. Other organizations use the books as a part of a systemwide learning program—supported by video and other media based on the content in the books. Still others work with Crisp Learning to customize the material to meet their specific needs and reflect their culture. Regardless of how it is used, we hope you will join the more than 20 million satisfied learners worldwide who have completed a *Fifty-Minute Book.*

Preface

Imagine calmly and confidently approaching the employer of your dreams, stating your professional qualifications and desire to work for that organization, and—*just like that*—walking away with the job you have always wanted.

OR

Picture yourself calling on a cold sales prospect who has never done business with your company and—*just like that*—closing the meeting with a big order on the books and a fat commission check in your pocket.

If these scenarios sound impossible, chances are you have not yet mastered the art of successful networking. If, on the other hand, you begin to develop your relationship-building skills and apply the proven networking techniques outlined in this book, you too may find yourself achieving the professional and personal success you have only dreamed of.

That is not to say you can become a successful networker and achieve accompanying career growth overnight. On the contrary, successful networking is a long-term strategy that calls for clearly defined goals, a detailed action plan, and an ongoing commitment to relationship building and career development.

This book is written to help you find your professional and personal focus, establish realistic and worthwhile objectives, chart your career course, and achieve the networking success and career growth you desire.

Nancy Flynn

Nancy Flynn

Dedication

To my husband, Paul Schodorf, the most important member of my network.

Contents

Introduction

Successful networking involves more than just making contacts. It depends on developing and following a strategic networking plan to fit your career and personal goals. There is no one-size-fits-all process. Certainly there are standard tools, techniques, and tips you can—and should—apply. But in the end, *your* strategic networking plan will be as unique as you are and as specific to your goals as possible.

As you progress through the exercises and discussion points in this book, you will have the opportunity to define clearly your networking style—and develop your one-of-a-kind strategic networking plan.

Your customized plan will be designed to maximize your professional and personal strengths while minimizing your weaknesses. Networking style considerations include:

> **Goals**—Your reasons for enhancing your networking skills

> **Contacts**—Your access to the "right" people at the right time

> **Personal style**—Your comfort level and listening skills and the impression you make

> **Tools and techniques**—Your experience and comfort level with publicity, public speaking, e-mail, and other networking tools

> **Resources**—Your ability to devote time, energy, and financial resources to networking and career development

> **Etiquette and netiquette**—Your know-how and savvy can make, or break, the deal

> **Challenges**—Your personal and professional problem areas

> **Commitment**—Your desire to succeed and willingness to follow through

Begin by taking the self-assessment on the next two pages to help you clarify your networking strengths and weaknesses, needs and goals.

ASSESSING YOUR NETWORKING SKILLS

For each of the following statements below, check (✔) the response that you think best fits. Be realistic as you look at your strengths and weaknesses. Most likely you will find you already have some networking skills and will discover other areas that need to be explored or fine-tuned.

Identifying Focus and Setting Goals

	Yes	No	Don't Know
1) I have a clear vision of my career goals.	❏	❏	❏
2) I have created a strategic networking plan to help me achieve my career goals.	❏	❏	❏
3) I am willing to invest the time, energy, and financial resources necessary to achieve my networking and career goals.	❏	❏	❏

Relationship-building Skills

4) I have established relationships with key influencers who can help me achieve my career goals.	❏	❏	❏
5) I have compiled a target list of influencers, mentors, colleagues, and supporters with whom I want to build mutually beneficial networking and business relationships.	❏	❏	❏
6) I am actively involved in professional organizations and/or alumni associations that can help advance my career goals.	❏	❏	❏

People Skills

7) I am an introvert. I find it difficult to introduce myself to strangers and make small talk at social events.	❏	❏	❏
8) I am an extrovert. I can talk to anyone, anywhere, about anything. Public speaking is a pleasure for me.	❏	❏	❏

═══CONTINUED═══

Networking Tools & Techniques	**Yes**	**No**	**Don't Know**
9) I would be comfortable using publicity to enhance my business profile and advance my career.	❏	❏	❏
10) I am an expert on at least one subject and would enjoy giving speeches on that topic.	❏	❏	❏
11) I have access to e-mail and the Internet and am comfortable using them.	❏	❏	❏
12) I am mindful of the rules of social, business, and e-mail etiquette, or *netiquette*.	❏	❏	❏

Networking Challenges

	Yes	**No**	**Don't Know**
13) I am a student or recent grad with no professional contacts.	❏	❏	❏
14) I am attempting to switch careers, start a business, or get my career back on track following a career setback.	❏	❏	❏
15) I am a top-level executive searching for a hard-to-find, high-paying position.	❏	❏	❏

Do not worry about how many *yes* or *no* answers you gave. As you proceed through this book, each topic will be detailed with examples and exercises to help you develop and implement the strategic networking plan that is right for you. Use your self-assessment to determine which networking skills you need to focus on most.

Understanding Successful Networking

2

Establishing Contacts with a Purpose

Networking is the indispensable art of building long-term, reciprocal relationships with the "right" people. Who are the "right" people? They are not necessarily the wealthiest, most powerful, or most senior executives in town. On the contrary, they are the people who—regardless of corporate rank or social position—understand how the networking game is played and are willing to help you get into the action and score a career goal.

In short, networking is reaching out and holding on to people who can make things happen—in a fraction of the time it would take you to accomplish the same goals on your own. As an example, fully 95% of human resource professionals and job seekers claim networking is the most effective tool to locate job candidates or secure a job.[1]

As a successful networker, you will learn to establish and grow relationships with people who can open doors, make introductions, and advance your career. Whether your goal is to secure a promotion, get a new job, go back to work after a termination or voluntary absence, promote yourself or your favorite cause, sell services or products, build a business, serve on a corporate or not-for-profit board, or become a celebrity within your industry, market, or community—your ability to cultivate contacts can make the difference between success and failure.

Networking Is a Two-Way Street

In the world of networking, your success as a receiver is directly proportional to your generosity as a giver. Take a "me, me, me" approach to networking, and you will be met with limited success. Be generous with the information you share, and you will find people equally willing to open doors, offer tips, and make introductions. Two-way networking involves several key activities:

> ### Sharing information and contacts with others

Although a job lead, contact, or other information may not be beneficial to you, it might be solid gold to someone else. Do not hoard information. The individual you help today could recommend you for your dream job tomorrow.

> ### Introducing people

Networking is all about people helping people. The more people you introduce, the wider your circle of influence.

> ### Doing favors

It takes only a minute to share a name, pass along a lead, make an introduction, or invite a colleague to an association meeting—but the residual benefits can last a professional lifetime.

> ### Asking for help

As your reputation as a giver grows, you will become increasingly comfortable asking for referrals, introductions, mentoring, and other assistance. Do not hesitate to make requests. People cannot help you unless they have a clear understanding of your networking needs and career goals.

> ### Acknowledging support

Thank the people who help you. A thank-you card or a small gift can leave a lasting impression—and help build valuable, long-term relationships.

Avoiding Networking Pitfalls

As important as knowing what networking *is*, is knowing what networking is *not*. The people who are most successful at establishing contacts are those who avoid the following pitfalls:

➤ **Failing to reciprocate**

Develop a reputation for taking help but never lending a hand, and you will quickly find your networking pool drying up.

➤ **Failing to acknowledge your network**

Careers ebb and flow. Snub the people who helped you on your way up, and you will likely be snubbed on the way back down. Successful networking is about nurturing long-term relationships, not using people for a quick career fix, then moving on.

➤ **Underestimating your contacts**

Some people are so busy trying to position themselves among the business elite—those with the most impressive titles, credentials, or degrees—that they are completely blind to the valuable contacts to be made among subordinates, suppliers, and co-workers. Do not be a relationship snob. The college intern you mentor this summer could turn around and introduce you to the CEO of a multinational corporation (who just happens to be her uncle) next fall.

Networking Nugget

Think twice before turning down a request for assistance, particularly if you could quickly or easily fulfill it. The person you help today could become a valuable addition to your networking circle—and invaluable should you one day need a favor.

Sharpening Your Networking Focus

Becoming a successful networker does not require being the most extroverted person in town—people skills can be learned. But it does require focusing clearly on your career goal and a networking strategy to take you there. The more directly you can focus on a specific career goal and accompanying networking plan, the more quickly you will achieve success.

Once you identify clear career goals, you will stop pursuing no-win business relationships and agonizing over inappropriate career choices. As a focused networker, you will pursue only the networking activities, business relationships, and professional skills that will move you closer to your career goals.

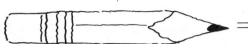

FORMULATE YOUR NETWORKING STRATEGY

This exercise will help you sharpen your focus. If you have more than one career goal, feel free to repeat this exercise for each goal. Be careful not to dilute your focus by pursuing too many goals simultaneously.

List your primary career goal. Be as specific as possible. Rather than the vague statement, "I want a new job," focus on details. Address as many of the *five Ws*—who, what, when, where, why—as possible. For example: "By January 1, I want to be a pharmaceutical sales representative, working in Chicago and making $75,000 a year."

_____

_____

_____

_____

List six specific actions (stick with non-networking activities for now) you can take to make your goal a reality. For example, "I will send five re-sumes a week until I have contacted every pharmaceutical manufacturer in the Midwest." Or, "I will take evening classes at State University in pursuit of a master's degree in chemistry."

1. _____

2. _____

3. _____

4. _____

5. _____

6. _____

List any challenges or obstacles you may face as you work toward your goal—for example, "I was laid off from my last sales job" or "I have no sales experience."

1. _____

2. _____

3. _____

List all the networking activities you can engage in to help you overcome your challenges and attain your career goal. For example, "I will ask my former sales manager to write a letter of recommendation explaining that my layoff resulted from corporate downsizing, not poor performance." Or, "I will contact the Chicago branch of my college alumni association for a calendar of meeting dates and social events."

1._____

_____

2._____

_____

3._____

_____

4._____

_____

5._____

_____

6._____

_____

7._____

_____

8._____

_____

P A R T 2

Building
Networking
Relationships

Cultivating Existing Contacts

If you already have established relationships with key influencers who can help you achieve your career goals, congratulations. If not, this section will help you identify people you already know whose help you may not have thought to tap. And you will learn ways to help you reach beyond your comfort zone and make new contacts.

Remember to include your spouse, family, neighbors, and friends in your networking circle. Think about what they do for a living, what hobbies they enjoy, what career paths they have followed, and so on. Use your next family gathering to find out where your cousins work, with whom your father-in-law plays golf, what challenges your self-employed aunt has overcome to build a successful business.

Follow the same line of questioning with your neighbors and friends to ensure everyone is aware of one another's expertise, experience, and goals. Discovering previously unknown connections within the group is both fun and potentially rewarding.

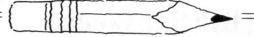

NETWORKING WITH PEOPLE YOU KNOW

The following exercise will help you identify the influencers, colleagues, supporters, and suppliers you already know—and with whom you may be able to build mutually beneficial networking relationships.

Step 1: In the spaces below, list current contacts who would be valuable networking partners for helping you work toward your primary career goal. For example, you might include a college professor, former supervisor, company alumni, executive director of a professional association, and so on.

Step 2: Write a brief script that summarizes your networking request and why you are making it. Be polite and bear in mind that successful networking is a two-way street. For example:

Contact's Name:	Bridget Schodorf
Relationship to You:	College Roommate
Script:	"Bridget, I recall your brother Tim is a sales manager with XYZ Pharmaceuticals. I'm looking for a job as a pharmaceutical sales rep. Do you think Tim would be willing to give me some career advice? May I have his phone number and mention your name when I call? I appreciate your help. Please let me know if I can return the favor."

Contact's Name: _____

Relationship to You: _____

Script: _____

_____

_____

_____

Contact's Name: _____

Relationship to You: _____

Script: _____

_____

_____

_____

Expanding Your Networking Circle

More often than not, you will be required to reach beyond your existing—and comfortable—contacts to maximize the effectiveness of your network and achieve career success. But the objective of networking is not merely to meet new people and move on. Your goal is to establish and grow long-term relationships based on reciprocity—"I'll help you today, and someday when I need help, you'll be there for me."

Just as you have created a process for cultivating current contacts, so too must you prepare to meet new people. List all the activities, events, locations, and organizations that would put you in direct contact with the "right" people—people who can help make your career goals happen.

In other words, where are you likely to run into the right people?

1. _____
2. _____
3. _____
4. _____
5. _____
6. _____
7. _____
8. _____
9. _____
10. _____
11. _____
12. _____
13. _____
14. _____
15. _____
16. _____
17. _____

Compare your answers to the author's suggestions in the Appendix.

Scripting Your 30-Second Self-Introduction

To take the edge off new situations and make the prospect of meeting strangers more comfortable, develop a networking script to introduce yourself. Think of your script as a 30-second "elevator speech." If you had only half a minute to tell a stranger who you are, what you do for a living, what your career goal is, what you have to offer, and how the listener can help, what would you say?

Shoot for three short yet descriptive sentences designed to break the ice, introduce yourself, and—ideally—fuel a longer conversation. For example:

Example A:

"Hello, I'm Nancy Flynn, a professional speaker and the author of several books including The *ePolicy Handbook* and *Writing Effective E-Mail*. I'm flying to Pasadena today to conduct a workshop on managing e-mail overload. How much e-mail do you send and receive each day?"

Analysis: Airplanes—particularly weekday flights when business people are traveling—are terrific for networking. Make a point to succinctly introduce yourself to the traveler(s) sitting next to you on the plane or at the gate. Close your introduction with an open-ended question that calls for more than a yes or no answer. You just may land a new client, a new job, or a valuable new member of your networking group.

Example B:

"Hello, I'm Nancy Flynn, a networking consultant and the author of Crisp Publications' *Networking for Success*. I conduct networking workshops to help business people make valuable contacts and land their dream jobs. If you know any job hunters who are having a tough time finding just the right position, have them visit www.WriteToBusiness.com for a list of upcoming seminars."

Analysis: In three short sentences, the speaker communicates who she is and what she does, while casting a net for additional clients, including the listener or the listener's contacts.

Example C:

"Hello, I'm Bridget Schodorf, a professional dog walker with 15 clients in this building, including a Chihuahua, a Great Dane, and just about everything in between. Executives who love dogs but are too busy to walk them twice a day really appreciate the personal attention I give my canine clients. Are you a dog lover or a cat person?"

Analysis: Not only does the speaker introduce herself and establish credibility ("Fifteen of your neighbors rely on me to walk their dogs"), but also she opens the door for a lively debate on the merits of cats vs. dogs.

Elevator Speech Do's and Don'ts

When composing your own 30-second elevator speech, be mindful of the following do's and don'ts:

Do:

➤ Focus on the task at hand. Look the listener in the eye and give the impression that, to you, the listener is the only person in the room.

➤ Introduce yourself, then listen attentively to your contact's introduction. Follow up with questions designed to get your contact talking about his or her career or interests. We all like to talk about ourselves. Focus your initial conversation on your contact, and you will be well received and remembered as a good conversationalist.

➤ Politely excuse yourself and move on once it becomes clear that, for whatever reason, this person simply is not a good networking contact for you. Your goal is to establish a few top-notch business relationships, not amass a large pool of so-so contacts. Do not run yourself ragged joining every industry association or attending every fund-raising event in town. Remain focused on your career goal. Strive for a small number of long-term, mutually beneficial networking relationships with people who can move you the farthest distance in the shortest amount of time.

Don't:

➤ Downplay your accomplishments. You only have 30 seconds to capture the listener's attention. Make your introduction memorable. Give the listener a reason to continue the conversation or remember you the next time you meet.

➤ Sound as though you are reading a script. Write and rewrite your elevator speech until it sounds just right. Then rehearse—first in front of a mirror, then with friends and family—until your three-sentence introduction flows as naturally and comfortably as possible.

Draft Your Own Elevator Speech

Write your own half-minute introduction. Use no more than three concise sentences to break the ice, introduce yourself professionally, and create an opportunity to stay in touch with the listener.

_____

_____

_____

_____

_____

_____

_____

_____

_____

_____

_____

_____

_____

_____

Preparing for Networking Events

Now you have learned the importance of breaking out of your comfort zone to expand your networking circle. You have brainstormed a list of places you might make new contacts, and you have developed a networking script for introducing yourself to people you do not know.

Among the best places to use this script are at events designed specifically for networking, such as professional association meetings and trade shows. Remember, successful networking is strategic networking. Before you rush out to that next business event, take some time to prepare for the people you hope to meet.

Develop a Target List

Review the group's membership roster or guest list and identify a handful of people you want to meet or renew acquaintanceship with. Networking success is about quality of contacts, not quantity. Especially if you are shy, setting a goal to talk to specific people will motivate you to break out of your shell and initiate a conversation.

If you have six people on your networking target list, try to learn something about each one before the event. Take a look at the target company's annual report or other company literature, so you can ask informed questions about the company.

Contact the target's administrative assistant before the event. Explain that you are hoping to chat with the executive at an upcoming professional event and would appreciate any insights that would help you break the ice.

Use your networking circle. Ask if anyone will be attending the event and would be willing to introduce you to the target.

Prepare to Meet Your Targets

Before the event, practice your 30-second elevator speech. Remember, use no more than three sentences to break the ice, introduce yourself professionally, and create an opportunity to stay in touch with the listener.

When you arrive, take a few minutes to get your bearings after entering the room. Center yourself. Scan the room for familiar faces and networking targets. Quickly devise a plan for working the room, based on your overall networking goals and target list.

Keep business cards handy for graceful distribution. Carry an empty card case to collect cards. Take a pocket calendar, so you can schedule interviews, follow-up calls, and lunch meetings. But leave your resume, portfolio, and other cumbersome material at home. Keep your hands free to shake hands and hold a beverage. You want to project a professional, in-control image. It is tough to do that when you are balancing stacks of papers.

Work the Room

When you are finally face-to-face with your networking target, ask for help clearly and specifically. The more specific your request for help, the more memorable. Rather than saying, "I'm looking for a marketing position," say "I'm seeking a position with an international marketing firm with a presence in the Far East. I speak Japanese and am willing to relocate abroad."

Spend no more than 10 minutes with each contact. Ask questions that demonstrate your awareness of the contact's company and your professional expertise. Then move on; do not get stuck.

If you find yourself engaged in a long conversation with someone other than a networking target, or if an introverted acquaintance is clinging to you, extricate yourself quickly and politely. Stay true to your networking goal.

Nurturing Your Support System

Expanding your network involves more than just meeting new contacts. To maintain your circle, you also must nurture those contacts by staying in touch. Do not just walk away from a positive encounter. Follow up a valuable connection with a handwritten note and business card. Or send an e-mail with an attention-getting subject line in which you mention a mutual acquaintance, extend a lunch invitation, or refer to a memorable comment made during your first encounter.

Keep your contacts in the loop. When a contact arranges a job interview, let the contact know where the interview process stands. Reciprocate whenever possible by making introductions or referrals for your contacts.

When a member of your networking circle does you a favor, no matter how big or small, be sure to say thank you. If a contact makes an introduction, writes a letter of recommendation, or otherwise takes action that results in business for you, send flowers, a book, or tickets to a sporting event—something to show your sincere appreciation.

Other ways to express your appreciation to mentors and networking contacts include the following:

➤ Nominate your mentor for a community or industry award (Communicator of the Year, for example).

➤ Offer your contact tickets to business, social, cultural, and sporting events. If you hold season tickets to the ballet but cannot attend a performance, give your tickets to a member of your networking circle. If you have been asking the right questions and listening carefully, you should know who would most appreciate receiving your tickets.

➤ Purchase an extra ticket (or perhaps an entire table) for a high-profile business, civic, or industry luncheon or dinner. Invite your most valuable contact(s) as your guest(s).

➤ Send birthday cards. Everyone sends holiday cards, but few business people send birthday cards. This is a great opportunity to distinguish yourself.

Finding a Mentor

The right mentor—an experienced, well-positioned professional with the contacts, willingness, and time to help you achieve your career goals—can be instrumental to networking and career success. Identifying, securing, and cultivating a mentor should be part of your strategic networking plan. Take these steps to help you find the ideal mentor for you:

1 **Schedule informational interviews.** Create a target list of people in your industry or profession who have achieved the kind of career success you desire. Call each to schedule an informational interview. Explain that you are interested in developing a career in the same field and would appreciate any time the individual is willing to give.

2 **Take advantage of the opportunity to learn.** Prepare for your meeting by compiling a list of questions. In what kind of work do you specialize? How long have you worked in your profession? What are the greatest challenges you faced early in your career? What advice would you give a fledgling professional? Stay away from questions the interviewee is likely to find inappropriate or too personal. Do not ask for client names or salary details. You are trying to make a contact, not an enemy.

3 **Develop your sales pitch.** Before you meet, spend time thinking about your strengths and what you have to offer a mentor. Do not approach anyone until you can succinctly and persuasively answer the question: "Why should I take time to mentor you?"

4 **Listen actively for clues.** During your informational interview, listen to the expert you have sought out. Do not waste time crafting a clever response when you should be listening.

5 **Be persistent.** If the executive you have targeted is too busy to mentor you right now, create ways to stay in touch. Send news clippings and magazine articles of interest. Send an occasional "just checking in" e-mail. Once a quarter, ask if mentoring is now a possibility or if your target knows another experienced professional who might be willing to work with you.

6 **Know when to walk away gracefully.** No matter how great your desire to work with an individual, if the mentor you have selected just isn't interested, you must walk away gracefully.

7 **Seek a reputable mentoring program.** Check with your local chamber of commerce and area business associations to see if they offer a mentoring program that will put you in contact with successful business people in your industry or community.

8 **Consider hiring a professional coach.** As an alternative to a volunteer mentor, a professional coach can act as your mentor/networking guide/career counselor all rolled into one. To locate a professional coach, start by visiting the International Coach Federation at www.coachfederation.org, or the National Speakers Association at www.nsaspeaker.org.

APPEAL TO YOUR PROSPECTIVE MENTOR

Finding a mentor begins with identifying likely candidates. List three
prospective mentors and what each has to offer you.

Name   **Why Would This Person Be a
                                  Valuable Mentor?**

1. _____   _____

2. _____   _____

3. _____   _____

Draft your mentoring sales pitch. Use no more than six sentences to
succinctly and persuasively answer the question: "Why should I take time
to mentor you?"

_____

_____

_____

_____

_____

_____

_____

_____

_____

_____

_____

_____

_____

23

Networking for Success

P A R T 3

Refining Your

Professional

Presence

Making a Positive First Impression

First impressions count, especially in business situations where you want to convey a professional image and be remembered as a serious contender for the job you are seeking or the business you are promoting. Fair or not, most of us take about 10 seconds to form an impression of a new acquaintance. Fortunately, there are steps you can take to ensure that the immediate impression you make is a positive one.

Consider Your Appearance

Incorporate dress and grooming into your strategic networking plan. Before heading out the door to an event where you are likely to encounter current or prospective members of your networking circle, check yourself in a full-length mirror. Is your overall look a positive selling tool, or does your appearance undercut your talents and abilities?

As a rule, you want to dress for the position you want, not the job you currently hold. That does not mean you should go into debt buying expensive clothes and accessories. It means you should make the most of what you have to work with.

Never underestimate the impact of facial expressions and body language. Introduce yourself with a smile and know that you are communicating a sense of friendliness and approachability. Maintain eye contact while conversing, speak in a friendly tone, and keep an open posture with arms at your sides.

Shake Hands with Confidence

In business situations, a handshake often is your first contact point with another individual. Your handshake says a lot about you, and helps others form immediate and lasting impressions of you. Keep these pointers in mind:

➤ In general, reserve handshakes for business situations. If you strike up a conversation with the person sitting next to you at a soccer game or the individual waiting next to you to board a plane, chances are you won't shake hands. When you introduce yourself or strike up a conversation at a trade show, professional association meeting, or fund-raising event, however, you will want to shake hands.

➤ Offer your hand equally to men and women.

➤ Make eye contact, smile, and exchange pleasantries ("Nice to meet you," "I've been looking forward to meeting you," "What a beautiful scarf") while you shake.

➤ Make full hand-to-hand contact. Extend your entire hand, not just your fingers.

➤ Offer a firm, friendly shake. A limp, lifeless shake projects a passive image. Pump too aggressively and you will come off as domineering. Large men should be particularly careful not to crush the hands of women and smaller men.

➤ Reserve two-handed shakes for friends or for individuals for whom you have genuinely warm feelings.

Turning Small Talk into Big Business

You will walk into any networking situation with more professional presence if you develop a conversational game plan beforehand. Be prepared with at least three pieces of small talk—light conversation that you can have with anyone you meet. The idea of small talk may make you cringe, but it is absolutely essential to networking. It is a way of learning about other people and finding mutual areas of interest. Applying the following basic rules of effective conversation will help you master the art of small talk.

Small-Talk Rule #1: Parrot, or repeat, the speaker's comments.

To demonstrate you are listening to and interested in the other speaker, use the parroting technique. For example:

Speaker: *"Our employees' personal use of company e-mail prompted us to implement an e-mail policy."*

Listener: *"An e-mail policy?"*

Speaker: *"Yes, the policy spells out exactly how employees may and may not use the company's e-mail system."*

Listener: *"So it specifically states what employees may write?"*

Speaker: *"Yes, for starters, we banned the use of all obscene, harassing, and menacing language."*

Small-Talk Rule #2: Ask open-ended questions to uncover valuable networking information.

Avoid yes/no questions. Asking open-ended questions allows you to develop a conversational string. Examples:

"What type of business are you in?"

"What is your position with the company?"

"What motivated you to get into that line of work?"

"What is the most rewarding aspect of your job?"

"What advice would you give a college grad looking to establish a career in your industry?"

"How are the job prospects within your industry?"

"What are the top five companies you recommend I contact?"

Small Talk Rule #3: Be observant.

Simply by observing others, you can pick up clues that will help you initiate conversations about your networking targets' interests. Examples of conversation starters stemming from observation:

"Your ring is beautiful. How did you get started collecting antique jewelry?"

"I see you have a Phi Beta Kappa key. Where did you attend college?"

"You are wearing a tie with my alma mater's logo. What was your major?"

"I see you ordered a meatless meal this evening. How long have you been a vegetarian?"

Conversational Do's and Don'ts

So far, you have checked your appearance, mastered your handshake, practiced your 30-second elevator speech, and are prepared to initiate small talk. At this point, people are often stymied at the prospect of what to say next—or of saying the wrong thing—as the conversation continues. Review these do's and don'ts to converse with ease.

Do:

➤ Stick with topics that are appropriate for the situation. If you attend a social event, keep the business talk to a minimum. Otherwise, you will look needy and will scare off networking prospects.

➤ Keep business conversations professional and topical.

➤ Read newspapers, newsmagazines, and trade publications to keep up-to-date on current events and industry news. Pepper your conversation with interesting facts, figures, and news nuggets.

➤ Ask open-ended questions to get the other person talking. Indicate your interest with eye contact, body language, and follow-up questions.

Don't:

➤ Flirt, curse, repeat off-color jokes, gossip, brag, or use turn-off language that will paint a negative picture of you and send the listener running.

➤ Ask questions designed to elicit a yes or no answer.

➤ Monopolize the conversation or interrupt other speakers.

➤ Look around the room when you should be listening to—and making eye contact with—the speaker.

➤ Ask personal questions or comment on potentially embarrassing matters (a divorce, the loss of a job, a lawsuit, etc.).

➤ Continue a conversation with an individual who indicates no interest in you or in whom you have no networking interest. Excuse yourself politely and move on.

Mastering the Art of Listening

Being a good conversationalist includes being a good listener. That is why networking success depends as much on how well you listen to the other person as on what you actually say. Effective listening is a learned art. Masterful listeners "seduce" speakers: When the conversation ends, speakers are left with positive feelings about themselves and about the listeners. Follow these do's and don'ts for masterful listening:

Masterful Listeners Do:

➤ Make and hold eye contact with the speaker. Nothing says "I'm listening" more effectively than eye contact.

➤ Give the speaker feedback. Facial expressions, body language, gestures, questions, and comments assure the speaker the listener is involved.

➤ Maintain a pleasant expression, giving no sign of impatience or eagerness to "work" the room. Focus 100% on the speaker.

Masterful Listeners Don't:

➤ Interrupt the speaker. Positive feedback is one thing; interruptions are another. Interruptions tell the speaker "I know more than you do" or "Your comments just aren't important to me."

➤ Worry about their response. If you are busy mentally rehearsing responses or questions, you are likely to miss the speaker's comments. Often speakers are not looking for a response; they simply want to be heard. That is the job of a good listener.

➤ Impose their own agenda on the speaker. A networking situation is not necessarily the time for a heated debate. You do not have to agree with everything the speaker has to say, but you are obligated to listen attentively. If the speaker's comments are inappropriate or offensive, excuse yourself and cross this individual off your networking list.

➤ Turn off and tune out the speaker. Whether you are scanning the room for better contacts or simply thinking about other matters, why strike up a conversation if you are not going to listen?

Projecting Your Image on Paper: Business Cards

Most networking opportunities end with an exchange of business cards. This practice gives you one more way to connect with your contact, communicate your career goal, establish a networking relationship, and make a positive, professional impression.

If you are currently employed, business cards are a breeze. Just be sure to have a supply on hand in all business situations and whenever and wherever networking opportunities are likely to arise. If you are between jobs, produce your own business card. The goal is to look as if you are working even when you are not. Follow these guidelines:

Business Card Do's:

➤ Project a professional image. White card stock and black ink are your safest choices, depending on your industry. Colored cards stand out more and are often used in creative fields, but they may scream amateur in more conservative industries. If your budget allows two-color printing, make black your primary color and use a businesslike color (blue, red, green) as your spot color.

➤ Focus on readability. Use large type and plenty of white space. Make your name and contact numbers jump off the card.

➤ Create a title, such as "sales professional" or "career coach," that describes your experience or career goal and place it under your name where a job title would go.

➤ Use the front of the card to provide comprehensive contact information: your name and address, phone and fax numbers, e-mail address, and Web address. If you post a resume online, you may want to note it, such as "Resume available at www.WriteTo Business.com."

➤ List a phone number(s) where you can be reached. Use a home phone number only if you have a second line dedicated solely to business and networking, you live alone, or you control how the phone is answered or what voice mail message is played during business hours. Provide a cell phone number only if you carry it and keep it turned on.

➤ Keep your business cards handy and distribute them freely. As a conversation draws to a close, pull out your card and say something along the lines of, "I appreciate your advice today. Why don't I give you one of my cards. If you hear of an opening that's right for me, please give me a call. And may I have your card too?"

Business Card Don'ts:

➤ Don't cram too much copy onto both sides of the card. Use the front of the card to communicate important contact information, and think twice before printing on the back. You do not want to come off looking desperate. You simply want to give your networking contact an easy way to remember and reach you.

➤ Don't include a photo of yourself unless you are a professional speaker, actor or model, or work in an industry where it is customary to do so. First impressions affect hiring decisions. Do not give a prospective employer the opportunity to dismiss you from a reaction to your photo.

➤ Don't use a photo more than five years old. If you use a photo at all, have it professionally shot and keep it current.

➤ Don't list your degree unless you are a Ph.D. or M.D., a recent grad with no other qualifications, or a job hunter whose degree is necessary for the job.

➤ Don't leave home without your cards. Be prepared with clean cards ready for easy distribution.

➤ Don't be offended if someone declines to accept your card. Just scratch this person off your networking list and move on.

Bell-Ringing Telephone Techniques

Identifying Key Contact Points

Whether your goal is to land a promotion, secure a new job, win a seat on a corporate board, attract clients to your small business, or become a celebrity within your market or industry, your success is directly related to your ability to make contacts and build mutually beneficial relationships with the right people.

The avenues through which you might initially make contact and eventually build valuable relationships include six key contact points:

> ➤ Meetings and events, business and social

> ➤ The telephone

> ➤ E-mail and the Internet

> ➤ Snail mail

> ➤ The media

> ➤ Speaking engagements

You have already learned from Part 2 about making contacts at meetings and networking events. In this part you will learn about networking via the telephone, including voice mail. Subsequent chapters of this book discuss the other avenues.

Cultivating the Gatekeeper

Next to meeting face-to-face, the telephone can be an unbeatable networking tool—provided you can get past the gatekeeper.

Unlike e-mail, which 96% of executives read and respond to personally,[2] almost all business people rely on a gatekeeper to screen their incoming phone calls. In some cases, two screeners—a receptionist and an executive assistant—determine which calls get through.

What is the secret of telephone success? Cultivating the gatekeeper. Follow these guidelines:

➤ Ask the receptionist the name of the administrative professional who screens calls for the decision-maker. Ask to speak with that individual, not the executive.

➤ Show an interest in the gatekeeper. Address the gatekeeper by name and ask how the day is going.

➤ Demonstrate your respect for the gatekeeper's position and power by presenting your need and asking for advice or help. For example, "Gina, I would like to meet with the chief financial officer to discuss your organization's accounting and auditing needs. I know the CFO has a demanding schedule. How would you suggest I go about securing an introductory appointment?"

➤ Consider working directly with the gatekeeper and bypassing the executive altogether. Some executives assign enormous responsibility to their assistants. Once you present your need and ask for help, you may be pleasantly surprised to learn the assistant has the power to handle your request.

➤ Never talk down to or disrespect a gatekeeper—unless you want word of your rudeness to get back to the decision-maker.

➤ Always thank the gatekeeper who helps you.

Gatekeeper Relations: Dream or Nightmare?

There are many ways to treat the administrative professional who serves as the gatekeeper to the decision-maker you need to reach. How you come across to that gatekeeper can often make—or break—your chances of getting through and doing business with that organization, as you will see in the following extreme, though entirely conceivable, scenario.

> *A vice president with a well-funded charitable organization, Deidre was a high-profile executive who was on a first-name basis with every CEO and major donor in town. Because her position gave her direct access to decision-makers, Deidre never thought it necessary to cultivate gatekeepers. On the contrary, she had no respect for administrative assistants and was blind to the power they often wield. One day, while awaiting an appointment with the CEO who served as her organization's board chairman, Deidre made the career-altering mistake of rudely dismissing the CEO's assistant. Within hours, Deidre's boss received a phone call from the CEO, complaining about the treatment his assistant of 25 years had received, and permanently banning Deidre from his offices. Shortly thereafter, Deidre was terminated from her position.*

The example of Diedre may be the worst-case scenario, but it illustrates what can result from disrespecting the gatekeeper. Now consider what would happen if the gatekeeper were treated, not just with respect, but as someone in a position of power—the power to put you through to the decision-maker. The following example portrays the success that can come from cultivating the gatekeeper.

> *An experienced salesman, Roger always made a point of chatting with the administrative professional on the other end of the phone line. Not content just to learn a name, he would spend a few minutes at the beginning of every phone call trying to make a personal connection with the gatekeeper. If the prospect was located in Wisconsin, for example, Roger would mention he attended college in that state, then inquire how long the gatekeeper had lived in Wisconsin. While chatting, Roger would jot notes (name, interests, education, etc.) on index cards, which he kept by his phone and referred to before making follow-up calls. Unaware that Roger was using cheat sheets, the gatekeepers he spoke with invariably were wowed by Roger's memory and personal interest. As a result, Roger's calls were quickly routed to decision-makers who typically had received advance notice of what a great guy Roger was.*

Create your own Networking Cheat Sheets using two sides of a three-by-five-inch index card. Staple additional cards as needed. Record the kinds of information listed below:

Front

Name _____

Title _____

Company _____

Gatekeeper to Whom _____

Phone _____

Fax _____

E-Mail _____

Web site _____

Best Day/Time to Call _____

Back

Date of Last Call _____

Topic of Last Conversation _____

Interests _____

Connections with Me _____

Education/Schools Attended _____

Family _____

Professional Memberships _____

Memorable Traits/Comments/Nuggets _____

Other _____

Introducing Yourself by Telephone

Whether speaking with decision-makers or administrative professionals, strive to make a powerful impression over the phone. Your initial two-minute phone conversation may determine whether you get in to see the decision-maker in person.

Success on the telephone, as in life, calls for preparation. Do not leave networking and career success to chance. Prepare brief telephone scripts to guide you through introductory conversations.

➤ Remember the 30-second elevator script you drafted earlier? Think of your telephone script as an extended version of that exercise. Your goal now is not only to introduce yourself, but also to provide the listener with the incentive to take whatever action you desire, such as schedule a face-to-face interview or request a sample of your product.

➤ Be mindful of the listener's time. Limit your introductory phone conversation to a maximum of two minutes. Ask questions to draw the listener into your conversation. Be an active and responsive listener.

➤ Draft your script as an inverted pyramid. Start with the good stuff— the information most likely to persuade your listener to stay on the line. Save the small talk or dry technical details for later in the conversation.

➤ Warm up the listener by dropping the name of a mutual contact or demonstrating your knowledge of the organization or decision-maker.

➤ Begin with a scripted 30-second conversation opener, and build your two-minute introductory phone call from there.

Sample Conversation Opener with Decision-Maker:

"My father, Michael Cull, tells me you and he worked together as copy boys at the Tribune early in your career. My goal is to land a newspaper job as soon as I receive my journalism degree, just as you and Dad did. Would you have 15 minutes to meet with me to discuss the current job market for young reporters? Afterward, I'd love to hear what my dad was like when you two were starting out together. And I'd be glad to fill you in on what he's up to now that he's working on the other side of the news fence as a publicist."

Analysis: By dropping Dad's name at the beginning of the phone conversation, this job seeker is positioned as an extended member of the decision-maker's professional family. By making her request for time brief (15 minutes) and offering to swap tales about Dad, the caller alleviates any concerns the decision-maker may have that the meeting will turn into a high-pressure pitch for a job.

The ideal scenario: The decision-maker takes the bait, talks briefly and fondly about his experiences as a copy boy, and schedules a face-to-face meeting as a favor to his old friend's daughter.

Sample Conversation Opener with Gatekeeper/Administrative Professional:

"I just finished reading a profile of Mrs. Wise in the State University alumni magazine. I was struck not only by her career history, but also by the value she places on your contribution to her success. Given her acknowledgement of and appreciation for your support, I wonder if Mrs. Wise would consider being my mentor. I have five years' experience in the industry now, and I would like to get some pointers from the first woman to make it to the top of our industry. Can you suggest how I might approach Mrs. Wise about mentoring me on a formal or informal basis?"

Analysis: By doing her homework and reading up on Mrs. Wise, the caller has uncovered a legitimate and effective connection to the gatekeeper. By mentioning the compliment Mrs. Wise paid her administrative assistant in the magazine article, the caller acknowledges the admin's status in the office and creates an opening to ask for help from this well-positioned individual.

SCRIPT YOUR TELEPHONE INTRODUCTION

Draft three separate 30-second telephone conversation openers, each customized to suit the specific listener outlined below:

1. **Script One:** Conversation opener with gatekeeper/administrative professional.

   _____

   _____

   _____

2. **Script Two:** Conversation opener with a cold decision-maker (one with whom you have no connection).

   _____

   _____

   _____

3. **Script Three:** Conversation opener with a warm decision-maker (one you know personally or through a member of your networking circle).

   _____

   _____

   _____

Networking Through Voice Mail

Answering machines and voice mail were cursed when they were first introduced onto the business scene. Now most people recognize their convenience and the technologies are here to stay. To use them successfully, apply the following tips and techniques:

For Outgoing Voice Mail

For many business people, voice mail is the gatekeeper of choice. They simply let the machine answer, then choose which calls to respond to. When you are faced with this electronic gatekeeper, apply the following strategies:

➤ Speak slowly. Do not rush though your message.

➤ Keep your message brief and to the point. Be prepared with a 30-second voice-mail message whenever you place a networking call.

➤ State your name slowly. Spell your name if there is any chance of confusion.

➤ State your phone number *slowly*. Then say it again *slowly*. Few things are more irritating than receiving voice mail messages from callers who fly through their phone numbers, once, forcing the listener to play and replay the message to catch the number.

➤ If you use a cell phone or e-mail pager, give those numbers too—slowly and repeatedly.

➤ If you have an e-mail address, offer it. If there is any risk of misunderstanding or confusion, spell out your e-mail address.

➤ If you operate a Web site to which you would like to expose the listener, leave that address too. Be sure to speak slowly; spell out a potentially troublesome address; and offer a clear, concise, and compelling reason why the listener should take time to log on to your site.

For Incoming Voice Mail

All your networking activity will have been in vain if decision-makers cannot reach you when the time comes. When you are not available to take calls in person and must rely on voice mail, apply these tips:

➤ Leave a clear, concise, professional message. Steer clear of cute, silly, or off-color messages.

➤ If you work from home or are using your house as your networking home base, consider adding a second phone line strictly for networking and business use. If you must share a line with family or roommates, negotiate an arrangement so that between the hours of 9 A.M. and 5 P.M., the message played is your professional voice mail greeting. Be sure you alone answer the phone live during those hours.

➤ Provide the caller with alternative ways to reach you. For example, list your cell phone or mobile phone number, e-mail address, or Web address.

➤ Return all calls promptly and politely. A message may not seem important, but you never know where your next great referral, job, or sale will come from.

Networking Nugget

Always practice proper telephone etiquette. Leave cell phones and e-mail pagers turned off during job interviews, business lunches, and networking events. If you forget and a call comes in, do not answer it. Your message will be waiting after your meeting. On a related note, never put a prospective employer or valuable networking contact on hold to answer your second line or respond to call waiting. This is what voice mail is for.

P A R T 5

Networking via

E-Mail and the

Internet

Reaching Your Contacts Through E-Mail

From customer service representatives and sales managers to administrative professionals and CEOs, nearly everyone uses e-mail to communicate today. North American business has experienced a 66% annual increase in workplace e-mail in recent years, with 1.4 trillion messages sent in 2001, up from 40 billion in 1995, according to the research firm International Data Corp.[3]

Aside from being a quick and convenient way to communicate, e-mail offers networkers an added benefit. Fully 96% of executives report reading and responding to their own e-mail.[4] That gives you, as a strategic networker, a path around the gatekeeper and straight into the decision-maker's electronic mailbox—perhaps.

Although nearly all executives read and respond to their own e-mail, many rely on administrative professionals to screen incoming e-mail (26%), delete e-mail addressed to the executive (29%), and ghostwrite e-mail responses under their executives' names (43%).[5]

Because you cannot be certain who will read your e-mail message—the executive or the gatekeeper—you must craft messages that capture reader attention and motivate appropriate action regardless of who the reader is.

A Cautionary Note for E-Mail Users

Before using your current employer's e-mail system to send resumes to competitors or communicate with members of your network, check out your organization's written e-mail policy. Nearly a quarter of employers, 24%, ban personal e-mail. Remember too that the boss may be reading every e-mail message you send or receive. Fully 62% of employers monitor workers' e-mail use. And 51% have disciplined or terminated employees for violating e-policy.[6] Do not lose your job while networking your way to a new career.

Formulating an Effective E-Mail Message

If you are going to add e-mail to your networking arsenal, be sure your messages are opened, read, and acted upon. Whether the e-mail is opened often depends on the subject line, but then the message itself also must communicate clearly and effectively. For best results, restrict each e-mail to one primary message—the one action you want the reader to take, such as to open and read your attached resume or schedule a job interview.

Write a Subject Line with Oomph

Writers often compose subject lines that are too vague, boring, or cute to be effective. With a little effort, you can learn to write subject lines that make your e-mail messages stand out. Follow these guidelines:

➤ State your message clearly, concisely, and descriptively. For example, a subject line that reads "Executive Position Wanted" does not have the impact of "Corporate Turnaround Expert Available."

➤ Incorporate contact names. For example, "Matt Kennedy Suggests We Meet."

➤ Steer clear of spammers' favorite subject lines. A legitimate e-mail, if accompanied by a subject line commonly used by spammers, is likely to be trashed.

Avoid Using These in Your Subject Lines	
Information	Great Opportunity
Just for You	Free Gift
Thank You	Read This Now
Have You Seen This?	
Any mention of sex, hot photos, adults only, weight loss, or moneymaking opportunities	

Compose Your Content with Care

Keep in mind that your e-mail message will be competing for your recipient's time with many, many other activities. So it is best to limit your networking message to a maximum of one screen page. If you need more room, add an attachment. Focus on your first three sentences. By the end of sentence three, the reader should have no doubt what your message is about, or what action should be taken. Use the balance of your e-mail to drive home the point you made so succinctly and effectively in the first three sentences.

Be sure to proofread your e-mail message before sending to ensure it contains nothing offensive. Appropriate e-mail content:

➤ Is free from jokes

➤ Is well-written and businesslike

➤ Is free from obscene or sexual language

➤ Is free from racial comments

➤ Contains no harassing, menacing, negative, or defamatory comments

➤ Is free from mechanical errors and structural problems

Format for Readability

With e-mail, your goal is to grab and retain the reader's attention. Maximize the impact of your messages by leading with the good stuff; incorporating plenty of white space; and using bullets, numbers, and other visual cues to guide your reader.

To draw attention to on-screen messages, or because of laziness, many e-mail writers use all uppercase letters. Bad idea. A message written in all caps is more difficult to read than one written in standard style. The human eye is accustomed to reading a mixture of uppercase and lowercase letters. When you draft e-mail in all caps, you run the risk of slowing down and annoying a reader. You also risk offending readers who may sense you are "shouting" at them.

Signing Off with a Signature File

Make it easy for e-mail recipients to respond—via e-mail or other means. Do not sign off with your name alone. Create a customized signature file complete with your company name and address, phone and fax numbers, e-mail address hyperlink, and Web address hyperlink. For example:

Nancy Flynn
Executive Director
The ePolicy Institute
2300 Walhaven Court, Suite 200A
Columbus, Ohio, USA 43220
614/451-3200 (phone)
614/451-8726 (fax)
experts@epolicyinstitute.com
www.epolicyinstitute.com

If you are not currently employed, create a title that describes your experience or career goal. For example:

Bridget Schodorf
Graphic Artist
100 Truman Lane
Santa Fe, NM 00000
000/000-0000 (phone)
000/000-0000 (fax)
bschodorf@bridgetart.com
www.bridgetart.com

Networking Nugget

When selecting an e-mail moniker or Web site address, steer clear of anything that is cutesy, off-color, or just plain unprofessional. Part of your networking strategy is to ensure that every contact point (e-mail, phone, face-to-face meetings) enhances your credibility and leaves a lasting, positive impression.

Read Receipts

Think twice before selecting the *read receipt* notification option in your e-mail program. Some readers may be offended that you do not trust them to open their e-mail. If you want to ensure your message is received and read, call the recipient with a heads-up that your electronic message has been sent.

WRITE A NETWORKING E-MAIL

Draft a one-page e-mail message, complete with a powerful subject line. Your message and subject line should move you a step closer to your primary networking or career goal. It could be, for example, a cover letter with a resume attached, an invitation to attend an industry event, a letter of introduction. Be sure to incorporate white space and visual cues to ensure your message is opened, read, and acted upon by the reader.

[e-mail format]

To:

_____

From:

_____

Subject: _____

[message]

_____

_____

_____

_____

_____

_____

_____

_____

_____

_____

_____

_____

Techniques for successful electronic communication can be found in *Writing Effective E-Mail* by Nancy Flynn and Tom Flynn, Crisp Publications.

Tapping into Online Alumni Networks

Many large companies, forced to downsize but eager to maintain contact with former employees, have established company alumni networks online. These networks can be a gold mine for people–currently employed or unemployed–seeking to make valuable contacts and pursue new opportunities. Some companies use their own online networks to rehire experienced and trusted former employees when hiring picks up again.

If you have worked for a company that hosts an online alumni network, take advantage of the opportunity to connect with former colleagues and supervisors. You may end up rehired by your old employer or receiving a tip that leads to a new opportunity.

To maximize the effectiveness of your online alumni network:

➤ Develop a strategic plan for staying in touch with former colleagues and supervisors following your initial contact. For example, set a goal of e-mailing one former associate a day or setting up one lunch meeting per month.

➤ Do not wait until you need a job to tap into your alumni network. Contact former colleagues before you need them. Touch base and build relationships in a pressure-free environment.

➤ Become a networking resource for former colleagues. Share leads and make introductions. Networking is a two-way street, whether conducted online or in person.

➤ Thank former colleagues who help you land an interview or secure a job.

➤ Stay in touch with your online networking circle even after you land a job. You never know when you may need help again.

➤ Never criticize your former employer. You may have no intention of returning to your old company, but your words nonetheless could come back to haunt you.

Welcome to My Web: Creating Your Online Presence

A Web site is a passive, yet highly effective, networking and promotional tool. If you have not yet done so, consider establishing a Web site to help advance your networking and career goals.

➤ Make it easy for prospective employers, clients, and networking contacts to find you online. Choose a simple and memorable Web address (perhaps your first initial and last name plus dot-com). Add your Web address to your business card, letterhead, resume, and any promotional literature you produce.

➤ Be sure your Web site is attractively designed, reads well, and is packed with the information visitors need to decide to hire you or take whatever action you desire. Depending on your networking and career goals, content might include your resume, professional biography, a list of services offered, testimonials from employers or satisfied clients, a professional photo (head shot), and contact information.

➤ Always include a hyperlink from your e-mail message to your Web site. Consider embedding a hyperlink in the body of the e-mail message and in your comprehensive signature file.

Surfing the Web for Networking Leads

The Internet can be a valuable networking tool. You can research prospective employers and customers, gather contact names and e-mail addresses, and in many cases get up-to-the-minute information about employment opportunities. A Web site review before a job interview or sales call can arm you with data necessary to ask informed questions and present yourself as a prepared professional. Besides Web surfing, you may add chat rooms, forums, electronic newsletters, and discussion lists to your online networking tool kit.

Chat Rooms

Online chat rooms enable you to conduct one-on-one or real-time conversations with people who share your career or networking goals, background, and interests. Locate appropriate chat rooms on the Web or download chat software, and get your e-conversation underway.

Online Forums

Hosted by America Online®(AOL) and other Internet service providers, online forums offer networkers the opportunity to participate in discussions related to their profession, industry, or niche. If you are interested in creating a profile as a subject-matter expert, forum hosts are always eager to find credible experts who can lead forums.

E-Newsletters

Targeted to professional peers in a given occupation, electronic newsletters are online publications that can offer you a platform for showcasing your expertise. Regardless of your industry or profession, chances are someone is publishing an electronic newsletter on that subject. E-newsletter editors typically are hungry for well-written articles to fill their pages. If you are a subject-matter expert and want to be positioned as *the* source of information on your topic, offer your writing services free of charge to the most highly regarded e-newsletters in your niche.

Discussion Lists

Also targeted to a specific audience, discussion lists are by subscription only. Subscribe to a list related to your networking or career interest, then participate in the discussion simply by e-mailing to the posting address. Make valuable contributions, and you will soon find your profile and credibility growing.

A list of online networking sites and resources is provided in the Appendix.

Netiquette Guidelines for Networkers

By nature, e-mail is a "cold" medium. Messages written and conversations held on-screen lack the warmth of face-to-face discussions and telephone calls, which benefit respectively from body language and intonation. Couple its coldness with the tendency of many writers to type messages quickly and in some cases thoughtlessly, and it is easy to see how e-mail can result in hurt feelings and misunderstandings.

Adhering to basic rules of *netiquette,* or online etiquette, as outlined below, can alleviate problems and help cast you in a favorable light.

➤ Beware hidden readers. If confidentiality is an issue, do not use e-mail. An inaccurate keystroke or the recipient's decision to forward your message could land your e-mail on dozens, hundreds, or even thousands of unintended readers' screens. So think twice before using your employer's e-mail system to touch base, for example, with an executive headhunter.

➤ Write as though Mom were reading. Regardless of the intended reader, write your message as if your boss, the media, or Mom were reading.

➤ Remain gender neutral. Your intended reader may be a male, but the ultimate decision-maker could be the female executive who receives a forwarded copy of your original message. Send a message full of masculine pronouns (he, his, him, etc.), and you may turn off female readers.

➤ Keep your employer's harassment and discrimination policies in mind. Sexual or racial harassment or discrimination lawsuits have resulted from employees sending improper internal and external e-mail messages. All electronic communication should adhere to the rules set forth in the organization's harassment and discrimination policies.

➤ Do not use e-mail to let off steam. Upset or angry? Compose yourself before composing your message. Once you hit *send,* your e-mail is on its way through cyberspace and probably cannot be retrieved.

➤ Do not mail to the world. Send e-mail messages only to readers with a legitimate need for your information. Mail to your group list only when it is appropriate for everyone on the list to receive the message. Do not reply to a message unless you have something to contribute. Send your resume to one appropriate executive, not to everyone with the title *vice president*.

➤ Copy with care. Address your message to the person whom you want to motivate to act, and send carbon copies strictly as a courtesy. Carbon copy recipients are not required to reply to messages, so do not be disappointed when a response is not forthcoming.

➤ Do not oversell your message. Just because you have the ability to mark messages *urgent* does not mean you should. Reserve the urgent classification for messages that demand immediate action.

➤ Ask permission to forward material. Forwarding content without the original sender's permission could be a violation of copyright law.

➤ Never use e-mail to fire employees or deliver bad news. Without the benefit of body language, facial expression, or intonation, e-mail is the worst way to deliver bad news.

➤ Avoid e-mail if there is any chance your message will be misunderstood. Your networking goal is to make contact and build relationships, not turn off readers.

➤ Bear in mind that although e-mail is a quick way to send a message, it is not necessarily an effective way to generate a quick response. The reader is under no obligation to open, read, or respond to your message. If you need a response now, pick up the phone or meet in person.

➤ Do not rely on e-mail to the exclusion of personal contact. Even in the age of e-mail, face-to-face relationship skills remain at the heart of long-term networking and career success.

Taking Time for Snail Mail

E-mail is a quick and convenient way to communicate. But it is not appropriate in every circumstance. When a contact takes valuable time to talk with you or otherwise offers help, always compose a hand-written thank-you note—and mail it the old-fashioned way via the postal service.

In the age of e-mail, hand-written notes and cards have become such a rarity that the mere act of sending one will help set you apart from the competition. A personal note written on distinctive high-quality stationery and sent via snail mail will leave a lasting impression.

The Networking Power of Self-Promotion

Tooting Your Own Horn

It is not possible to achieve networking success without committing a certain amount of money and a considerable amount of time to self-promotion. You must get out and spread the word about your services and capabilities. No one else is going to do it for you unless you put a professional publicist on your payroll.

Most people think publicity "just happens" to people who are so well known, well respected, and well spoken that the media naturally flock to them. On the contrary, publicity is the result of hard work, including phone calls placed to TV assignment editors, press releases mailed to print reporters, and e-mail messages sent to radio news directors. But the power of any resulting publicity—even a small item in your suburban or small-town newspaper—is enormous.

Self-promotion delivers four benefits that belong in the arsenal of all successful networkers:

➤ Increased exposure

➤ Enhanced credibility

➤ Perceived third-party endorsement

➤ Positioning as "the expert"

Do not be intimidated by the words *promotion* and *publicity*. And do not be put off by the idea of spending a few dollars to make considerably more. As you move toward your career goal, there will be many occasions when you will be required to invest in yourself.

You do not have to invest a fortune in self-promotion, and (except in extreme circumstances) you need not launch a full-blown public relations campaign. But you must do what you can to ensure your target audience knows who you are, how to find you, and why they should care about you. Successful self-promotion, like successful networking, results from setting goals, acting strategically, and applying a few tricks.

NAME THAT PROMOTIONAL TOOL

As you build your network and widen your circle of contacts, you will be able to rely more on word of mouth and less on self-promotion. Until you reach that point, however, it is essential that you launch—and maintain—an ongoing program to keep your name in front of the business community at large, along with any niche market (healthcare, law, high-tech, etc.) that you have targeted as a career goal.

List all the promotional tools you could use to help position yourself, broaden your networking circle, and achieve your career goal.

1. _____

2. _____

3. _____

4. _____

5. _____

6. _____

7. _____

8. _____

Compare your answers to the author's suggestions in the Appendix.

Spreading Your News in a Press Release

Whether your networking or career goal is to land a job, heighten your professional profile, or sell products and services, spreading your news to the media can help speed you toward your goal. And the basic tool for gaining the attention of the media is a *press release* that is well written and carefully targeted.

When is it appropriate to issue a press release?

➤ You have landed a new job.

➤ You have been promoted.

➤ You have been appointed to serve on a business, social, or community board.

➤ You have graduated.

➤ You have published a book.

➤ You are speaking publicly or conducting a workshop.

➤ Your company is introducing a new product or service.

You need neither a degree in journalism nor experience as a reporter or PR professional to write effective press releases. All you need are basic writing skills, an understanding of news hooks, and a willingness to learn.

Formatting Press Releases

Press releases are written in a specific, compact format so newspeople can quickly scan their content for newsworthiness. Every release should follow this basic format:

➤ Print press releases on plain white paper. Use an 11- or 12-point font, and maintain one-inch margins on all sides. Single spacing is fine, but double spacing maximizes readability.

➤ At the top of the page, print the date for the release to be distributed, or substitute the words *For Immediate Release*. List the name and phone number of a contact person who will be available should the media seek additional information. Never list a contact person who will be on vacation, in meetings, or otherwise unavailable the days immediately following a press announcement.

➤ Limit your press release to one page. Rarely is a two-page press release warranted. When an announcement is important or complex enough to require two pages or more, be sure to print "more" at the bottom of page one.

➤ Enhance readability by writing short sentences and tight paragraphs. Use bullets, dashes, or numbers to break copy into easy-to-scan blocks.

➤ Keep an eye on spelling, grammar, and punctuation. A press release that is riddled with mechanical errors—therefore tedious to read and unprofessional—likely will end up trashed, regardless of the story's merits.

➤ Signal the end of your press release with three spaced hash marks *(# # #)* or the number *-30-*.

Press Release Writing 101

Because the news business is deadline oriented, the media cannot afford the luxury of wading though half a page of extraneous information to get to the good stuff in your press release. Do not be a mystery writer. Use the *inverted pyramid* approach to ensure your press release gets off to a strong start. The most important information is communicated in the *lead,* with additional information following in descending order of importance.

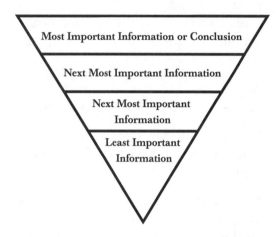

Most Important Information or Conclusion

Next Most Important Information

Next Most Important Information

Least Important Information

Lead Your Press Release to Success

Beginning with the first word of the first sentence and ending at the conclusion of the first paragraph, the lead is your best, and sometimes only, opportunity to grab the reader's attention. A well-conceived lead draws readers in, motivating them to read the press release to its conclusion. Keep these points in mind when crafting your lead paragraph:

➤ The lead structures your press release, so the media have no doubt what you are announcing or whether they should continue reading and cover your story.

➤ The lead delivers the release's most important, compelling facts–the *five Ws*–right up front, often in terms of a conclusion.

➤ The lead summarizes what is to come later in the release.

➤ The lead draws readers in, creating interest in your announcement and a desire to share the information with readers, viewers, or listeners.

Address the Five Ws

To ensure that your lead delivers your press release's most important information, answer the journalist's five Ws in the first paragraph:

Who: State who is making the announcement, explain who will be affected by the news, let reporters know whom they may contact for additional information. Most important, provide the answer to the question, "Who cares?" If you cannot think of a good reason that the media or public should care about this particular announcement, do not issue a press release.

What: Explain what the announcement is all about. Be specific. And provide the answer to a skeptical "So what?"

When: Provide event dates and times. If organization representatives will be available for interviews, let the media know when.

Where: Be specific. Give a street address and directions if your announcement revolves around an event or activity at a hard-to-find location.

Why (or How): This is the biggie. Why should readers, listeners, or viewers care about this announcement? Why are you taking the media's time with this press release? Why are you making the announcement now? How will area residents be affected? How can interested readers get more information?

Now you try it: Using the five Ws, draft the lead for a press release announcing a career accomplishment (a new position, promotion, appointment to a committee or board, etc.).

_____

_____

CASE STUDY: A TALE WITH TWO LEADS

Imagine you are an author ready to announce the publication of your new business book, so you decide to write and send a press release to relevant trade publications. The following two leads, each announcing the same news, include the five Ws in different ways. Now imagine yourself as the editor of a business publication and compare the leads for effectiveness. Then answer the questions that follow.

> Columbus, OH—Nancy Flynn, co-author of *Writing Effective E-Mail: Improving Your Electronic Communication,* is pleased to announce the publication of her fifth book, *Networking for Success.* Flynn's newest book, published by Crisp Publications, was written to help job hunters and business people enjoy unprecedented career success.

> Columbus, OH—What secret weapon do all successful job hunters have in common? Networking skills. Call it schmoozing, relationship building, or people skills—it all comes down to knowing the right people with the right connections to help you land the right job. Whether you are a recent college grad just entering the workforce or a senior executive looking for a six-figure position, your ability to network successfully can make all the difference. So says the author of the new book, *Networking for Success* (Crisp Publications, 2003), which helps job hunters and business people enjoy unprecedented career success.

Which lead would motivate you to read the rest of the release? Why?

_____

_____

What elements of your preferred lead might motivate an editor or reporter to develop a feature article on the topic? Why?

_____

_____

Compare your answers to the author's suggestions in the Appendix.

Writing Bylined Articles

Writing an article (or having it ghostwritten) and getting it published is a terrific, cost-effective way to position yourself and promote your expertise, services, or products. A 1,000-word bylined article costs nothing to run (unlike advertising), yet has enormous impact on readers.

As part of your networking strategy, pursue byline placements in newspapers, magazines, and newsletters read by your contacts, clients, and networking prospects. Approach the editors of your community's daily, weekly, and monthly business publications. Contact editors of trade magazines and newsletters that serve your target industries. Introduce yourself and offer to write a bylined article on a subject that would interest the publication's readers. Bylines are intended to inform and educate, so go heavy on advice, tips, and how-to information.

At the conclusion of the article, include a brief bionote with your name, firm name, phone number, e-mail address, and Web address. Some publications will even run your photo with the article.

Steps to Successful Byline Placement

1 **Brainstorm topics.** Develop articles that help readers achieve success, overcome problems, enhance profitability, or work smarter. Steer clear of topics that are nothing more than veiled attempts to promote yourself and your products or services. Bylined articles should be written to educate, not advertise.

2 **Do your homework.** Unless you have a specific publication in mind, research media directories and develop a list of publications that cover the industries or geographic markets important to you and your networking circle. Check out editorial calendars to determine if your article would work as part of a publication's special issue. If so, contact editors several months in advance of a special issue.

Media directories and other publicity resources are listed in the Appendix.

3 **Pick up the phone and talk with the right editor.** Call the publication and ask to speak with the articles editor. Establish yourself as a credible expert qualified to write the article. Ask if the editor is interested in discussing a bylined column on your topic.

4 **Explain, briefly and clearly, what your topic is and what the main copy points will be.** Think about the reader. Pepper your conversation with timely, interesting, and compelling facts and figures. Stress that the article will be written to educate the people who make up the magazine's readership, not to promote you.

5 **If the editor is interested, discuss details.** Ask how many words the editor wants and in what format (disc, e-mail attachment, e-mail in the field, or hard copy mailed or faxed). Confirm your deadline—and be sure to meet it!

Reprint Positive News Coverage

Whenever you appear in print via a press release or bylined article, clip the article, reprint it, and send it to your networking circle. Before doing so, however, check with the publication to ensure you are in compliance with copyright law.

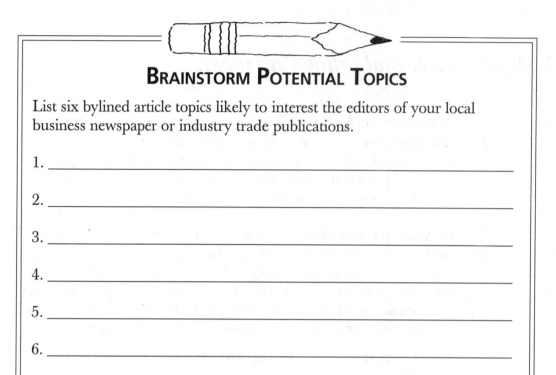

BRAINSTORM POTENTIAL TOPICS

List six bylined article topics likely to interest the editors of your local business newspaper or industry trade publications.

1. _____

2. _____

3. _____

4. _____

5. _____

6. _____

Compare your answers to the author's suggestions in the Appendix.

Putting a Face to Your Name

Many trade publications will include your photo with a bylined article, which helps increase your visibility in your industry. You also may accompany press releases with your photo, depending on the news being announced, such as a new position or promotion. Maximize the effectiveness of your photo by following these tips:

➤ Employ a professional photographer.

➤ Request a three-by-five-inch head shot and let the photographer know you will be using the photo for publicity purposes.

➤ Keep trying until you get a photo you are happy with. This is the face you will be showing the world when you cannot appear in person.

➤ Have both color and black-and-white prints made.

➤ Create a high-resolution scan, so you can e-mail your photo.

➤ Have a new photo taken at least every five years.

➤ Label the photo with your name, title, company name, phone, fax, and e-mail.

Promoting Yourself Through Speaking Engagements

Public speaking is a surefire way to elevate your profile and enhance your credibility, which is critical to networking and career success. Strive to match your speaking activity with your professional expertise. Give audiences what they want—a subject matter expert who can deliver timely advice and information to help improve on-the-job performance—and you will be on your way to speaking success.

You do not have to be a professional entertainer or a big-time celebrity to land on the speaking circuit. On the contrary, corporations, associations, and government entities are always searching for informative, articulate speakers to educate and entertain audiences. Professions that impose continuing education requirements on members (such as healthcare, law, real estate, and accounting) have an ongoing need for speakers who can help professionals perform their jobs more effectively, while meeting their continuing education requirements.

If you are reserved—more a teacher than an entertainer—do not despair. There is a real market for speakers with content to deliver who are hired to teach, not entertain.

Start Slowly, Grow Steadily

If your background includes experience teaching or speaking publicly in any way, standing in front of an audience may come naturally to you. If, however, you have no public speaking experience and the thought of standing up and speaking in front of a room full of strangers unsettles you, get some training before embarking on a speaking career.

Plenty of resources are available for novice speakers. Many universities and community colleges offer public speaking courses through their adult education programs. And in most major markets, you are likely to find a local chapter of the National Speakers Association (www.nsaspeaker.org), which offers comprehensive educational resources for speakers. Other good resources for fledgling speakers are Toastmasters International® (www.toastmasters.org) and Dale Carnegie Training® (www.dalecarnegie.com).

Learn by doing free programs for clubs, church groups, and school groups. Seek out organizations in small communities or suburban neighborhoods. Check your local daily and suburban newspapers to see what group is meeting and when. Then contact the head of the organization to offer your speaking services. Even in the early days of your speaking career, the key to success is to talk about what you know best and give audience members the information they need most. As your speaking skills and confidence grow, you can move on to professional and industry associations, business and civic groups, and other organizations through which you are likely to make valuable contacts.

Shout Your Speaking Success

Spread the word that you are available as an expert speaker. Issue press releases when appropriate. If you are speaking to a garden club, an announcement in the local suburban news would be appropriate. If your venue is a national industry conference, let the trade magazines serving that industry know when, where, and on what topic you will be speaking. Speeches often translate effectively into bylined articles. Every time you agree to a speaking engagement, ask the meeting planner if the organization publishes a newsletter or magazine for which you might submit an article.

START THINKING ABOUT SPEAKING

List three topics you could develop into hour-long speeches. Next to each, list three potential speaking venues. For example:

Topic	Venues
Marketing Your Dental Practice	City Dental Association
	State Dental Association
	City Dental Hygienists Association
Writing Effective E-Mail	Local Rotary Club
	City Bar Association
	Statewide Sales Club

1. _____   _____

   _____

   _____

2. _____   _____

   _____

   _____

3. _____   _____

   _____

   _____

Volunteering for Networking Success

One effective way to position yourself before and demonstrate your skills to the right people is through volunteer service to professional, civic, arts, and charitable organizations. Unlike your personal volunteer work, which is most likely a labor of love, your professional volunteer activities should be approached strategically. Before deciding where to offer your time and expertise, consider the following points.

Do Your Homework

Most organizations produce an annual report or publication that lists executives, board officers, and members. Target the organization(s) that offer access to people on your networking contact list. Typically, the boards of arts organizations and other not-for-profit groups are peopled by the most powerful CEOs in town. This is your opportunity to meet, work with, and wow them.

Seek High-Profile Involvement

Do not be just a passive member. Get actively involved and gain visibility by volunteering to serve on the committee most likely to put you in contact with the right people.

Demonstrate Your Skills

Put your unique skills to work to demonstrate how good you are at what you do. For example, if you are a writer, offer to edit the organization's newsletter. If you are an administrative professional, volunteer to update and maintain the group's database. If you are an executive, get involved in fund-raising.

Making the Most of Trade Shows and Conventions

Trade shows, conventions, conferences, and seminars give speakers and attendees alike the opportunity to meet and network with a wide group of people in a short period of time. Attend each event with the goal of making valuable contacts to add to your network. The following tips will lead you to that goal:

➤ Brush up your 30-second elevator speech. Here is a great opportunity to put it to work.

➤ Carry a supply of business cards. Keep them handy and ready for distribution.

➤ Introduce yourself to the people sitting next to you or standing around you.

➤ Introduce your contacts to others.

➤ Attend the cocktail parties, networking luncheons, and hospitality events hosted by the sponsoring organization and vendors.

➤ Stay at the event hotel to increase your chances of meeting people in your industry.

➤ Introduce yourself to speakers and high-profile industry executives you otherwise might not have access to.

➤ Smile and shake hands. Be approachable and warm.

➤ Address people by their names and ask plenty of questions. We all love to talk about ourselves.

➤ Follow up with a phone call, e-mail message, or face-to-face meeting as soon as possible, while your contact's memory of you is fresh and favorable.

Special Networking Challenges: Novices and Veterans

Recent College Graduates: Learning the Ropes

Even if you are a recent graduate with few connections and limited (or no) job experience, you can begin building your networking circle with the contacts you can make by associating with your school's alumni and professionals in the field or industry you are pursuing.

Networking with College Alumni

College graduates have access to a powerful networking circle in their college alumni association. According to collegegrad.com, more than 90% of active alumni are willing to help new graduates of their alma maters. Tap into this network by following these guidelines:

➤ Contact your school's alumni office to access its alumni database.

➤ Search for alumni who are working in your chosen field, for your target employer, or in your city or the market of choice.

➤ Develop a target list of alumni to contact first by phone or e-mail. Then follow up by snail mail.

➤ Schedule face-to-face informational and fact-finding meetings whenever possible.

➤ Attend local alumni association meetings in the city or region you are targeting—and get actively involved. The more involved and well known you become, the more willing people will be to help.

Networking by Association

Professional and industry associations can be a gold mine for recent college graduates looking to build or expand their networking circle. By joining—and actively participating in—the right professional associations, recent grads can expand their networks, meet prospective employers, and gain insight into hiring practices, corporate culture, and more. Follow these tips for successful networking by association:

➢ **Be selective**

Join only those associations that will put you in contact with the right people. Start by asking your mentor and other successful professionals what industry associations they belong to. For a comprehensive list of associations in your industry or geographic market, visit the American Society of Association Executives (ASAE) at www.asaenet.org.

➢ **Enjoy guest status before joining**

Many associations allow prospective members to attend a few meetings free of charge or at a reduced guest price. This is a great low- or no-cost way to determine whether an association is worth your time and money.

➢ **Take advantage of student discounts**

If you are still in school or are a recent grad, you may qualify for a student membership at a reduced cost. Just be sure to join the local association in your target market, not a campus-based, student-only branch of the association.

> ### Mine the membership directory

As an association member, you should receive a current membership directory—an invaluable networking tool.

> ### Approach prospective contacts and employers

Use the membership directory to reach out to prospective networking contacts or employers. Whether using e-mail or the phone, be sure to mention you are a student member of the association, are conducting a job search, and would like to schedule a brief informational interview.

> ### Cut your losses

Some association chapters are so overrun with students and job seekers that professional members—the people you want to contact—do not attend meetings. If you find yourself surrounded by dozens of people just like you (fresh out of college and looking for a job), cut your losses and move on. It is unlikely these people can help you find work.

Senior Executives: Searching the Hidden Job Market

Executive positions with six-figure salaries are more likely to be found through personal contacts than classified ads. In fact, according to studies by executive search firms, 70% of top executives find their jobs through networking.[7] To tap the hidden, top-paying job market, chief executive officers, chief financial officers, general managers, and other senior executives must hone their strategic networking skills by heeding the following do's and don'ts for high-powered job seekers.

Do:

➤ Take advantage of your severance package, stock options, and savings. Unlike workers who live paycheck-to-paycheck and must find a new job immediately, displaced executives often have the flexibility to conduct a lengthy and comprehensive search for just the right job.

➤ Contact other executives in your professional circle to let them know you are out of work and eager to make solid contacts who can help you land a new job.

➤ Contact senior executives who recently landed the kind of position you seek. Introduce yourself and ask the execs to share the secrets of their job search success.

➤ Make your job search a full-time job. Get up, get dressed, and get to work networking and looking for a new position every day.

➤ Maintain a high profile in your community and profession. Maintain top-of-mind awareness to keep job leads coming your way.

➤ Hone your elevator speech: three descriptive sentences that are designed to break the ice, introduce you, and—ideally—fuel a longer conversation.

➤ Pass on leads you cannot use to other out-of-work executives.

➤ Join a senior executive networking forum in your community or industry. This is your opportunity to share war stories with and pick up tips from other top-level job seekers.

➤ Tap online alumni networks operated by former employers. People who once worked with or for you may now be able to help you secure a new position.

Don't:

➤ Let your ego get in the way of your job search. You may be used to calling the shots, but now you need to call on others to help you. Do not be embarrassed or reluctant to ask for help. The more clearly you articulate who you are, what you do for a living, what your career goal is, what you have to offer, and how the listener can help, the more likely help will be forthcoming.

➤ Go underground. Never has it been so important for you to attend events–business, professional, civic, and social–at which you are likely to make lasting contacts with the right people.

➤ Stop networking once you land a new job. Keep your networking circle alive and growing even after you have landed a new position. Maintaining contact and continuing to lend a hand to others will serve you well should you ever again find yourself out of work and looking for help.

➤ Forget to thank everyone who helps you on your way back to the top.

A P P E N D I X

PUTTING IT ALL TOGETHER:
CREATING YOUR STRATEGIC NETWORKING PLAN

This is your opportunity to create a one-of-a-kind strategic networking plan based on the exercises and activities covered in this book. Think of your strategic plan as your personal networking roadmap to a successful future.

1. Identify your primary career goal. Be as specific as possible.

   _____

   _____

2. List any challenges or obstacles you may face as you pursue your career goal.

   _____

   _____

3. List all the networking activities you can engage in to help overcome challenges or obstacles and attain your career goal.

   _____

   _____

4. List all current networking contacts that can help you achieve your career goal.

   _____

   _____

5. List any prospective or target contacts who can help make your career goal a reality.

   _____

   _____

6. List all the networking activities that would put you in contact with valuable prospective networking partners.

   _____

   _____

CONTINUED

7. Write your 30-second, three-sentence elevator speech.

_____

_____

8. Name three current or prospective career mentors.

_____

_____

9. List three specific actions you can take immediately to put your strategic networking plan into action.

_____

_____

To ensure networking success, assign yourself the task of completing at least one networking activity each workday. Assign yourself 10 networking activities or assignments to be accomplished over the next two workweeks. Check off (✔) tasks as they are completed.

Day	Task	Completed (✔)
Monday	_____	❑
Tuesday	_____	❑
Wednesday	_____	❑
Thursday	_____	❑
Friday	_____	❑
Monday	_____	❑
Tuesday	_____	❑
Wednesday	_____	❑
Thursday	_____	❑
Friday	_____	❑

Author's Suggested Responses

Expanding Your Networking Circle (Page 13)

Professional, industry, and trade associations

Chambers of commerce

Civic associations

College alumni associations

Neighborhood associations

Professional and business seminars and workshops

Online alumni associations

Airplanes and airports

Commuter trains

Social events

Business luncheons

Elevators

Sporting events

Golf courses

Hobby-related gatherings

Online chat rooms and e-mail

Public speaking

Name That Promotional Tool (Page 64)

Write and distribute press releases.

Write and place bylined articles in business and industry publications.

Write letters to the editor.

Write and submit editorials to newspapers—dailies, weeklies, trades.

Contribute articles to newsletters.

Make yourself available as an expert source for media interviews and as a source of background information.

Give speeches and conduct training.

Volunteer to serve on targeted boards and committees.

Attend industry trade shows.

Publish a newsletter.

Get your name and photo in the news.

Case Study: A Tale with Two Leads (Page 69)

The first lead begs the question, who cares? It may appeal to the author and her close friends and family, but it means nothing to anyone else. The press release probably would not be published anywhere but in a local neighborhood newspaper or perhaps in an association newsletter. Effective press releases do more than deliver facts. They deliver facts with style.

The second lead, by contrast, states the conclusion right up front, giving the media all the ingredients of a potential story. Any editor, reporter, or broadcast producer interested in covering employment trends might decide to develop a story based on *Networking for Success*.

Brainstorm Potential Topics (Page 72)

Topics that have worked well for the author over the years:

> *E-Mail: Keep It Clean, Make It Snappy*
>
> *10 Tips for Effective—and Safe—E-Mail*
>
> *The ABCs—and P's & Q's—of E-Mail*
>
> *E-Mail Is No Excuse for Bad Writing*
>
> *Good Legal Writing Is Plain English*
>
> *Selling Your Ideas Through Persuasive Writing*
>
> *Writing Effective Memos*
>
> *Tips for More Effective Web Sites*
>
> *Empower Your Business Writing*

Resources for Successful Networking

Associations

American Society of Association Executives
202-626-2723
www.asaenet.org

Encyclopedia of Associations
Gale Group
27500 Drake Rd.
Farmington Hills, MI 48331-3535
248-699-4253
www.galegroup.com

Coaching

International Coach Federation
1-888-423-3131
www.coachfederation.org

Publicity

Bacon's Media Source (Media Lists)
Bacon's Information, Inc.
1-800-621-0561
www.baconsinfo.com

Public Speaking

Dale Carnegie Training
www.dalecarnegie.com

National Speakers Association
480-968-2552
www.nsaspeaker.org

Toastmasters International
1-800-993-7732
www.toastmasters.org

Online Networking Sites

There are thousands of online networking, career, and job-search sites. A few of the author's favorites are listed here. Use these sites to link to other online networking resources.

E-Groups

www.egroups.com
This free service allows you to create and join e-mail groups, a convenient way to connect with others sharing interests and ideas. The business and finance page is a go-to networking tool.

Fast Company Community of Friends

www.fastcompany.com/cof
In *Fast Company* magazine's network of discussion groups, mentoring, and networking organizations, you can meet people associated with your industry. Build a personal profile online. Use your digital business card to connect, communicate, and collaborate.

Ask the Head Hunter.Com

www.asktheheadhunter.com
Q&A with an executive recruiter, plus articles on networking and job-search strategies.

Internet FAQ Archives

www.faqs.org
Read about newsgroups and most commonly asked questions.

Google Groups

http://groups.google.com
Search for newsgroups.

Comprehensive Networking and Career Information

www.careerknowhow.com
www.collegegrad.com
www.schmoozemonger.com/links.htm
www.usatoday.com

Recommended Reading

Networking

Bonet, Diana. *The Business of Listening*. Menlo Park, CA: Crisp Publications, 2001.

Fisher, Donna. *Professional Networking for Dummies*. NY: Hungry Minds, Inc., 2001.

Mackay, Harvey. *Dig Your Well Before You're Thirsty*. NY: Currency Doubleday, 1997.

Misner, Ivan R. and Don Morgan. *Masters of Networking: Building Relationships for Your Pocketbook and Soul*. Atlanta: Bard Press, 2000.

E-Mail and Internet

Flynn, Nancy and Tom Flynn. *Writing Effective E-Mail: Improving Your Electronic Communications*. Menlo Park, CA: Crisp Publications, 2003.

Publicity

Begley, Kathleen. *Writing That Sells*. Menlo Park, CA: Crisp Publications, 2002.

Flynn, Nancy. *The $100,000 Writer: How to Make a Six-Figure Income as a Freelance Business Writer*. Boston: Adams Media Corporation, 2000.

Public Speaking

Caroselli, Marlene. *Thinking on Your Feet*. Menlo Park, CA: Crisp Publications, 1992.

Mandel, Steve. *Effective Presentation Skills*. Menlo Park, CA: Crisp Publications, 2000.

Paulson, Terry. *50 Tips for Speaking Like a Pro*. Menlo Park, CA: Crisp Publications, 1999.

Walters, Lilly. *Secrets of Successful Speakers: How You Can Motivate, Captivate, and Persuade*. NY: McGraw-Hill, 1993.

How to Book a Networking for Success Seminar or Speaker

Author and speaker Nancy Flynn offers *Networking for Success* workshops and speeches based on the material presented in this book. The author of several books including *Writing Effective E-Mail* (Crisp Publications), Ms. Flynn is an internationally recognized expert who has been featured by *The Wall Street Journal, US News & World Report,* USAtoday.com, National Public Radio, *Woman's Day,* and thousands of other national and international media outlets.

Ms Flynn is founder and executive director of The ePolicy Institute, an organization devoted to helping reduce electronic risks and enhance e-mail writing and management skills. Through the ePolicy Institute Speakers' Bureau, Ms. Flynn conducts seminars worldwide on e-mail writing, e-mail management, and e-policy.

To book a *Networking for Success* workshop or keynote speech, or for information about ePolicy Institute seminars, contact Ms. Flynn:

Nancy Flynn
Author, Speaker and Consultant
www.WriteToBusiness.com
Executive Director, The ePolicy Institute
www.ePolicyInstitute.com
2300 Walhaven Court, Suite 200A
Columbus, OH 43220
Toll Free: 800-292-7332   Phone: 614-451-3200   Fax: 614-451-8726
E-mail: Nancy@WriteToBusiness.com
E-mail: Nancy@ePolicyInstitute.com

Notes

[1] Society for Human Resource Management and Careerjournal.com 2001 survey. Reported by www.careerknowhow.com. Survey results available at www.shrm.org/surveys or www.careerjournal.com.

[2] International Association of Administrative Professionals (IAAP) and The ePolicy Institute Online Poll, January 23, 2002.

[3] Elizabeth Weinstein, "Help! I'm Drowning in E-Mail!" *The Wall Street Journal,* January 10, 2002. Article available online at www.epolicyinstitute.com.

[4] IAAP and The ePolicy Institute Online Poll.

[5] Ibid.

[6] American Management Association, *US News & World Report,* ePolicy Institute *2001 Survey of Electronic Policies and Practices.* Survey results available at www.epolicyinstitute.com.

[7] Kate Berry, "The Bigger They Are, The Harder They Fall," *Orange County Register* article published in *The Columbus Dispatch,* January 13, 2002, sec. E, p.2.

NOTES

100

NOTES

Networking for Success

CRISP WORLDWIDE DISTRIBUTION

English language books are distributed worldwide. Major international distributors include:

ASIA/PACIFIC

Australia/New Zealand: In Learning, PO Box 1051, Springwood QLD, Brisbane, Australia 4127   Tel: 61-7-3-841-2286, Facsimile: 61-7-3-841-1580
ATTN: Messrs. Richard/Robert Gordon

Hong Kong/Mainland China: Crisp Learning Solutions, 18/F Honest Motors Building 9-11 Leighton Rd., Causeway Bay, Hong Kong   Tel: 852-2915-7119,
Facsimile: 852-2865-2815 ATTN: Ms. Grace Lee

Indonesia: Pt Lutan Edukasi, Citra Graha, 7th Floor, Suite 701A, Jl. Jend. Gato Subroto Kav. 35-36, Jakarta 12950 Indonesia Tel: 62-21-527-9060/527-9061 Facsimile: 62-21-527-9062 ATTN: Mr. Suwardi Luis

Japan: Phoenix Associates, Believe Mita Bldg., 8th Floor 3-43-16 Shiba, Minato-ku, Tokyo 105-0014, Japan   Tel: 81-3-5427-6231, Facsimile: 81-3-5427-6232
ATTN: Mr. Peter Owans

Malaysia, Philippines, Singapore: Epsys Pte Ltd., 540 Sims Ave #04-01, Sims Avenue Centre, 387603, Singapore   Tel: 65-747-1964, Facsimile: 65-747-0162 ATTN: Mr. Jack Chin

CANADA

Crisp Learning Canada, 60 Briarwood Avenue, Mississauga, ON L5G 3N6 Canada
Tel: 905-274-5678, Facsimile: 905-278-2801 ATTN: Mr. Steve Connolly

EUROPEAN UNION

England: Flex Learning Media, Ltd., 9-15 Hitchin Street,
Baldock, Hertfordshire, SG7 6AL, England
Tel: 44-1-46-289-6000, Facsimile: 44-1-46-289-2417   ATTN: Mr. David Willetts

INDIA

Multi-Media HRD, Pvt. Ltd., National House, Floor 1, 6 Tulloch Road,
Appolo Bunder, Bombay, India 400-039 Tel: 91-22-204-2281,
Facsimile: 91-22-283-6478 ATTN: Messrs. Ajay Aggarwal/ C.L. Aggarwal

SOUTH AMERICA

Mexico: Grupo Editorial Iberoamerica, Nebraska 199, Col. Napoles, 03810 Mexico, D.F. Tel: 525-523-0994, Facsimile: 525-543-1173   ATTN: Señor Nicholas Grepe

SOUTH AFRICA

Corporate: Learning Resources, PO Box 2806, Parklands, Johannesburg 2121, South Africa, Tel: 27-21-531-2923, Facsimile: 27-21-531-2944 ATTN: Mr. Ricky Robinson

MIDDLE EAST

Edutech Middle East, L.L.C., PO Box 52334, Dubai U.A.E.
Tel: 971-4-359-1222, Facsimile: 971-4-359-6500   ATTN: Mr. A.S.F. Karim